by Laurie Beckelman

Series Consultant
John Livingstone, M.D.

Crestwood House
Parsippany, New Jersey

Depression

For the friends who listen —
Siri, Shelley, Winnie, and Ro

Author's Note: Many teenagers generously shared their thoughts and
experiences with me. The quotes in this book are based on their stories.

Published by Crestwood House, an imprint of Silver Burdett Press.
A Simon & Schuster Company
299 Jefferson Road, Parsippany, NJ 07054

First Edition

Design: Lynda Fishbourne, Hemenway Design Associates
Packaging: Prentice Associates Inc.
Photos:
Superstock: (P.R. Production8)Cover, 8, 13, 15, 24, 27,
PhotoEdit: (Gary Connor)4,(Richard Hutchings)17, (James Shaffer)22,
(David Young-Wolff)30, (Robert W. Ginn)36, (Michael Newman)41,
Image Bank: 35,44,46.

Printed in the United States of America
10 9 8 7 6 5 4 3 2 1

Library of Congress Cataloging-in-Publication data

Beckelman, Laurie
    Depression / by Laurie Beckelman — 1st ed.
        p. cm. — (Hot line)
    ISBN 0-89686-845-1   ISBN 0-382-24956-9 pbk.
    1. Depression, Mental — Juvenile literature. 2. Depression in
    adolescence — Juvenile literature.   [1. Depression, Mental.]
I. Title. II. Series.
RC537.B425   1995
616.85'27—dc20   94-30976

Summary: A discussion of depression and how it differs from the everyday blues. Offers
suggestions for understanding and managing depression and for recognizing the signs of
depression in oneself or one's friends.

Depression

C O N T E N T S

*Some days,
Sherri felt so
blah that life
lost all its color.
On others,
sadness covered
her like a
leaden blanket.
Sometimes she
felt a frighten-
ing emptiness
and confusion
inside.*

Sherri, Tara, and a Bottle of Pills

Sherri pulled the strands of long, dark hair she was chewing out of her mouth. "Your hair isn't lettuce, and you're not a rabbit," she heard her mother's voice scold inside her head. But Sherri couldn't help herself. She was nervous. She chewed fiercely on a wad of hair and checked yet again for Tara's bus. Still not here. She *had* to see Tara, her best friend, before school started. She was really worried about Tara.

Sherri paced up and down in front of the school, thinking about the call she'd had from Tara the night before. Tara was in tears. She'd had a fight with her mom — nothing unusual about that. But Tara sounded weird. She was crying the way a baby cries, sobbing so hard that she was gasping for air. Tara tried to tell what had happened, but Sherri could barely understand her, so she just listened to Tara cry. When Tara stopped crying, she didn't tell Sherri her story. Instead, she said,

"Everything's fine now. You've been a great friend, Sherri, but I've got to go." Then she hung up. Definitely weird. Sherri called back, but the line was busy.

And now Tara's bus was late. Sherri pulled the hair out of her mouth. She checked her watch, then saw the bus finally pull up to the curb. She ran to meet it. She felt a great wave of relief when she saw Tara. Her friend was smiling and practically skipped over to meet her. Maybe everything *was* OK.

"I've got something to show you," Tara said excitedly, pulling Sherri over to the privacy of a big oak tree, "but you have to promise not to tell *anyone*."

"What is it?" asked Sherri, excitement replacing worry.

"Promise not to tell?"

"*Tara*! Of course I promise!"

"OK," said Tara, fumbling in her bag. "Look." Tara grinned as she held out a bottle of pills.

Sherri stared blankly at the pills. "I don't get it. What are they?"

"They're pills, silly. And I'm going to take them all."

Before Sherri could absorb what Tara had said, Tara slipped the pills back into her purse, gave Sherri a quick kiss on the cheek, and ran into school.

Sherri felt her knees go weak. Tara, her best friend, had just told her that she planned to kill herself, and she had made her promise not to tell.

*　*　*

As Sherri stood under that oak tree, she felt many things: panicked, shaken, worried, angry. But she also felt confused — not only about whether or not to break her promise to Tara, but also about Tara's pills. Why would Tara want to kill herself? They were best friends. They talked about everything: fights with parents and siblings, trouble with boyfriends, and the moods that seemed to come out of nowhere, making them listless or angry or ready to cry. Sherri *knew* Tara. Or at least she thought she did. She thought she knew how Tara felt and thought and what she was likely to do. But she never expected this.

As Sherri walked slowly toward school, she thought about her own bad moods. Some days, she felt so blah that life lost all its color. On others, sadness covered her like a leaden blanket. Sometimes she felt a frightening emptiness and confusion inside. When she would look at herself in the mirror, a stranger would be staring back. But all these feelings were like passing clouds. They came and went. She never wanted to kill herself — not even at the worst times, like when Jeff broke up with her and her pain was so deep and dreadful that she thought it would last forever. So how could she and Tara, who were so much alike, be so very different?

For some teens, the pale hues of the blahs give way to the deep midnight blue of despair. These teens become depressed.

Shades of Blue

There are many teens like both Sherri and Tara. Sherri's everyday blues and blahs are as normal a part of adolescence as first dates and MTV. Most teens — indeed, most people — experience them. In fact, researchers estimate that the average person feels down on three days out of ten.

Unfortunately, the hopelessness that Tara feels is not that uncommon, either. For some teens, the pale hues of the blahs give way to the deep midnight blue of despair. These teens become depressed. We use the word *depression* loosely in conversation to refer to anything from the down feelings Sherri has to Tara's despair and suicide plan. But doctors use the word more specifically to refer to a medical illness called **depression**. Throughout this book, we'll use the terms *the blues* or *depressed mood* to mean everyday moodiness and the term *depression* to refer to the illness.

According to the National Institute for

Mental Health, 1.5 million American children under 18 suffer from depression. This serious medical illness can lead to suicide. Although most people who become depressed do not commit suicide and not all suicides are because of depression, the link between the two is strong. This is just one reason why understanding the teenage blues and how they differ from depression is important. If you can spot the warning signs of depression (see page 38) in yourself or a friend, you can get help. Depression is a treatable disease.

But understanding the teenage blues is important for another reason, too. When we learn to recognize, label, and tolerate these normal feelings in ourselves, they do not seem as overwhelming. They are less likely to trigger the illness depression. What's more, by listening carefully to our blues, we can often learn more about ourselves, our relationships, and our needs. And when we know more about who we are and what we need, we're better able to make good choices in our lives.

Listening to the Blues

Many books about depression promise to tell you how to beat the blues. This one doesn't. While depression is an illness that should be treated, the blues are a normal part of life's ups and downs. They can be painful. They can be scary. They can hurt terribly. But they aren't bad. And they aren't feelings that should be avoided at all costs.

Too often, we learn from parents, television, peers, and others to bury rather than confront our uncomfortable emotions. We may have grown up with messages that convince us that these feelings aren't normal. Many adults are ill at ease with their own unhappy feelings and so may deny them in their children. Our parents or other adults may have laughed at our upsets, not taking them seriously because we were "just kids." Perhaps they denied our feelings, telling us that we weren't sad or unhappy when we said we were. Or maybe they tried to make them go away quickly by giving us a treat rather than listening to and accepting us. We may have learned to eat, drink, or shop our bad feelings away.

Parents or others may have made us feel bad about feeling bad. Perhaps you've heard lines like these: "I'm not taking a sourpuss to the movies." "There's no place for a mopey child in *this* house." "Come on now, big boys (or girls) don't cry."

Unfortunately, responses like these too often convince us that we "shouldn't" feel down. As a result, we bury these uncomfortable feelings, sometimes hiding them even from ourselves. But our feelings are like an inner tube. They are designed to help carry us safely down the streams of our lives. Push them down, and they'll just bob up again. They are trying to tell us something, and listening to them is important.

In order to listen to your blues, you have to be willing to stick with them awhile. This doesn't mean wallowing in them or playing them over and over like a broken record. It doesn't mean that you shouldn't do things to make yourself feel better. But it *does* mean not running when you see the blues coming. It means letting yourself feel the feeling, label it, and, perhaps, share it.

Some kids, not to mention adults, go to great lengths to keep the blues away. They find these feelings so awful that they dive into activity, any activity, to avoid facing

them. They may change something on the outside — friends, boyfriend or girlfriend — without first listening to the voices *inside* to make sure they're changing the right thing. Some even try to dull the blues with drugs, alcohol, or sex. But when the party is over or the alcohol has worn off, the feelings still remain.

None of these tactics is nearly as helpful as listening to the blues. Listening to your emotions is a skill. Like many others, it can be mastered over time. The "Tune In" chapters in this book offer suggestions that can help you learn to listen to your blues. The more you listen, the more clearly you will hear the melody of self-knowledge over the rhythm of the blues.

Sherri's Blues

Sherri sat in math class, feeling her mood grow darker and darker. She felt overwhelmed, unable to understand what was going on with Tara or what she should do about it. She felt responsible and neglectful. She was Tara's best friend — shouldn't she have known that Tara was upset enough to think about killing herself? She felt frightened and alone. The more these feelings grew, the worse she felt about herself. Sherri wanted to crawl into a hole somewhere and hide until everything was OK again.

Many of the feelings Sherri experienced as she sat in her math class are typical of the mix of emotions that can contribute to the blues. Sometimes the blues are simply a sense of sadness or a feeling of dullness, as if nothing can give us pleasure. But more often these feelings come along with a jumble of others. When we're down, we often feel overwhelmed by our responsibilities and cut off from other people. We may find ourselves, our relationships, and our lives lacking, yet we see no way of making these things better. Self-doubt, confusion, fatigue, loneliness, fear — they can all be part of the blues. So can many seemingly unrelated feelings and behaviors.

The blues can show themselves in unexpected ways. This is most true for teens who have learned that they "shouldn't" feel down. Tearfulness; fatigue; unexplained aches and pains, irritability, fear, or worry; self-doubt; and poor concentration can all be signs of the blues.

If you have the blues, these feelings don't last long. They may be with you for a few hours or on and off for a few days or even a week. But they won't be constant. For example, if you go to see a funny movie while you're blue, you'll probably feel better when you leave the theater. Or you might feel better just by talking to someone about something that interests you.

Just talking to someone can often make you feel better when you have the blues.

Tune In:

Blue Notes

"Blue notes" — a record of your moods and feelings — can help you recognize the telltale signs of a depressed mood in yourself. Recognizing and labeling your feelings is a first step in learning to manage them. Here are some formats to help get you started.

■ If you feel comfortable writing, keep a "Today I felt . . ." journal. Start each entry with the words "Today I felt . . ." and write as much as you want about the moods of the day and the events that triggered them. Write about how you felt physically as well as mentally. Were you tired? Did you have any aches and pains you can't explain?

■ A mood log is a quick way to track your moods. Get a small notebook or calendar and simply jot down how you feel each day.

■ Make a mood chart by copying the signs of the blues onto a sheet of paper. Whenever things feel "wrong" inside, take out the list and check off those items you are experiencing.

Review your blue notes every week or two. Over time, you'll most likely see a pattern to your blues. Then, the next time you're aching and tired and a little sad, the feelings might not seem so confusing. You'll have a name for them: the blues.

A mood log is a quick way to track your moods. Get a small notebook or calendar and simply jot down how you feel each day.

Trigger Points

Karen remembers what it was like for her in the days after she lost the class election. "I didn't care about anything," she says. "All I wanted to do was sleep. My friends would call and I'd make up some excuse why I couldn't talk. My mom would want to chat and I'd tell her I had to study. I felt so rejected and hurt — I couldn't face anyone."

Karen had a depressed mood that was with her on and off for about a week. This reaction to her loss was normal. Although the teenage blues sometimes seem to come out of nowhere, they are often triggered by an event in our lives. The event may be as major as moving to a new town or as seemingly minor as being snubbed by a popular kid in class. Chances are that the problem that triggers the blues will fall into one of three categories.

■ *Losses*: Breaking up with a boyfriend or girlfriend, the death of a pet, moving away from friends or family — even the loss of a favorite possession or a big disappointment — can trigger a depressed mood. The more major the loss, the worse the feelings are likely to be and the longer they are likely to last. Significant losses, such as the death of a loved one or one's parents' divorce, often bring on a period of grieving. Grieving is a lot like depression, but it is not an illness. It is a normal response to loss that usually lasts six months to a year.

■ *Fights*: Fights with parents, friends, siblings, or others can leave us feeling isolated and misunderstood. Sometimes those with whom we argue say hurtful things. Their words can make us doubt ourselves. "My dad really lays into me sometimes," says Gary. "He goes on about how I'm a lazy good-for-nothing who won't amount to anything. I play it real cool, man, like there's no way he can get to me. But inside? That's a whole other story. I end up feeling worthless."

■ *Failure and rejection*: These are major confidence busters. When we don't get a job we applied for or a place on the team, when a cute guy or girl ignores us or we flunk a test, we may question our worthiness or lovableness or our ability to make it in the world. We can get the blues.

Tune In:
Know What Triggers Your Blues

When you feel the blues coming on, ask yourself the following questions to figure out whether they've been triggered by a recent event in your life.

■ What's happened in the past few days or weeks to hurt me?

■ What losses, failures, or rejections have I experienced?

■ Have I fought with anyone recently?

■ What am I facing that feels scary or overwhelming?

You might want to write down your answers, speak them into a tape recorder, or talk things over with someone you trust. All these methods can help you clarify your thoughts. Just like knowing *what* you feel, knowing *why* you're feeling that way often makes uncomfortable feelings less scary and overwhelming. Figuring out why you're feeling as you are might take several days. Don't give up. If nothing "bad" has happened, think about good things that might have a downside. For example, Karen, the girl who lost the school election, might have felt blue even if she had won, but for different reasons. She might have worried that she wouldn't do a good job. Or, she may have expected winning to change her life, then been disappointed when it didn't. Accomplishments and new opportunities are often stressful and can surprise us by triggering bad feelings as well as good ones.

If you can discover something specific that has triggered your blues, you might be able to take action to change the situation — and your feelings. Ask yourself

■ Is there something in this situation that I can control?

■ If so, can I make changes that will help me feel better?

For example, Gary, the boy whose dad criticizes him for being lazy, can't control what his father believes. But he can control what *he* believes. He can do a reality check by asking himself

■ Do I get my homework done?

■ Do I meet my responsibilities at home, even if I don't do things on my dad's timetable?

■ Do I follow through on commitments I make to myself, my family, and my friends?

■ Do *I* feel lazy?

If Gary can answer yes to the first three questions and no to the fourth, chances are his father's perception has more to do with the father than with Gary. Sometimes adults who are on the go all the time forget that

Gary might not be a "lazy good-for-nothing," as his father unfortunately calls him, but he may be depressed.

it's not only OK but necessary to rest. Gary might try to find a calm moment to talk with his father, using some of the ideas suggested on page 34. Perhaps Gary can help his father see his point of view. But even if he can't, knowing how *he* feels about his work and rest habits can help Gary feel less insecure when his father criticizes him. Honestly sharing his feelings can help Gary, too. Even if his father doesn't listen, Gary can feel secure in knowing that he has done his part in trying to communicate. The rest is up to his dad.

Of course, if Gary almost never meets his responsibilities at home and in school and if he feels grungy, not good, when he's lazing around, he may have a more serious problem. He's not a "lazy good-for-nothing," as his father calls him, but he might be depressed.

When the Blues Come Out of the Blue

"**E**verything on the *outside's* goin' just fine, so why does the *inside* feel so bad?" asks José. "Some days I feel like I can't hold it together."

"The smallest thing can make me cry," says Marta. "Just play me a love song or show me one of those sentimental card commercials on TV. I'm mush."

Like José and Marta, most teens experience waves of the blues that seem to come out of nowhere or seem too intense for the event that triggered them, such as watching a TV commercial. Such feelings can be frightening because they seem irrational and unconnected with our lives. But they are connected — not to changes in your outside world but to ones inside.

Adolescence is a time of enormous change — not only for your body, which may seem to be "morphing" into adult form, but also for your mind and relationships. You are going through what **psychologist** Eric Ericson called an **identity crisis.** As you get to know your changing body, your changing mind, and your changing relationships, you are building a new sense of self. This won't be the last time you ask yourself, "Who am I?" But it is the first.

Any period of change and transition brings uncertainty and **stress.** And these feelings can trigger the blues. Sometimes, identifying and labeling the changes you're going through can help. Recognizing your feelings may not make them go away, but it can make them seem less frightening.

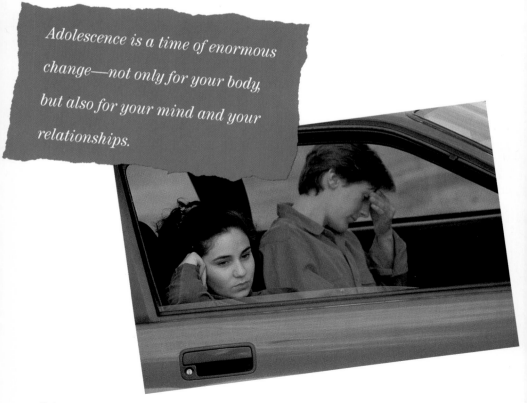

Adolescence is a time of enormous change—not only for your body, but also for your mind and your relationships.

Changing Bodies, Changing Minds

Change is to adolescence what wind is to air: It goes with the territory. First, take your body. Never again will it change so much so quickly. If your body hasn't started to change already, it will pretty soon. Everything from the size of your chest to the length of your nose to the quality of your skin will change. And you don't know how you'll end up looking.

These changes and the uncertainty they bring lead to very normal worries and self-doubt. Everyone's body develops at its own rate. For example, a girl who first gets her period at age 11 is normal. So is one who gets hers at age 15. But not all kids realize that "normal" is different for everyone. Some worry that they're developing too quickly. Others fear that their bodies will never grow. Some feel like strangers in their own skin. "It's weird," says Diana.

"Sometimes I don't look like me. I mean, I know it's me — I'm not crazy! — but I don't feel like me."

Doubts about looking good can be strong during the teen years because looking good takes on a new, sexual dimension. The physical maturity of **puberty** brings feelings of sexual arousal and aggression. Whether you find these feelings pleasant or troubling, they're new and bound to raise questions: Are your feelings normal? Are they too strong? Too weak?

These questions reflect the self-doubt and insecurity that are a natural part of coming to know oneself as a sexual person. Everyone has these concerns, but few people talk about them. We tend to feel weak and out of control when we admit our insecurities. Sometimes, we can't even admit them to ourselves. Yet facing self-doubt takes more strength than denying it. So does sharing our feelings.

The physical changes and doubts you may be experiencing are a lot to handle alone. And they're only part of the stress of adolescence because they're only part of the change. You're also thinking in new ways. You're now capable of what psychologist David Elkind calls "thinking in a new key." You can imagine the future and foresee the consequences of actions in ways you simply could not as a child.

Because you can imagine what you want to do with

your life, you may worry that you won't be able to fulfill your dreams. On the other hand, you may not yet know what those dreams are and may instead worry about that. This new thinking may leave you feeling really alone. For the first time, you may realize that you — not your parents or your friends — are responsible for yourself and your future. It's scary!

You may also find that problems beyond your control (for example, high unemployment rates, global warming, the threat of nuclear war) become more understandable — and more threatening. You may be concerned about the impact they could have on your own life.

For the first time, you may realize that you — not your parents or your friends — are responsible for yourself and your future. It's scary!

Tune In:
Take Care of Your Changing Body and Mind

The worries and insecurities of the age are normal, but they are also a source of stress on both your body and your mind. Stress affects our ability to cope. It can cloud your mind, making it harder for you to see your way out of the blues. Keeping your body and mind in good shape helps you cope with stress and therefore with the blues. To take good care of your body and mind, you need to

■ *Get regular check-ups*. Regular medical check-ups assure that you are healthy. They also give you a chance to share concerns about your body with a doctor or nurse. Find a doctor or nurse you trust and with whom you feel comfortable.

■ *Get rest*. Growing bodies need time to rest, and expanding minds need time to think. Napping, daydreaming, and lazing around listening to music can all be healthy responses to the stresses of adolescence.

■ *Exercise*. **Aerobic exercise** decreases tension and increases energy. It also may increase the levels of brain chemicals that have a good effect on mood. One study of depressed teens found that those who exercised felt less depressed than those who didn't.

■ *Make relaxation part of your life*. **Relaxation techniques,** such as deep breathing, **meditation**, or **yoga**, can also dissolve tension.

■ *Make pleasure part of your life*. Doing things you enjoy, even though you're feeling down, can help you feel better. Once your mood lifts a bit, you may be in a better frame of mind to come up with solutions to problems that were bothering you.

■ *Avoid alcohol and drugs*. Alcohol and many drugs are **depressants**. They will make you feel worse, not better.

■ *Avoid thought traps*. Thought traps are habits of thinking that make you feel less in control of your life, more worried, and more blue. Some thought traps to watch out for: negative self-talk ("I'm so stupid."); jumping to conclusions ("Paul didn't call. He hates me."); exaggerating ("Angel didn't return my call. No one *ever* calls me back."); worst-case thinking ("If I don't make the team, I'll *never* play basketball again."); globalizing

Napping, daydreaming, and lazing around listening to music can all be healthy responses to the stress of adolescence.

("I had a fight with my parents. *Everything*'s going wrong."); and self-centered thinking ("My mom's in a bad mood. I must have done something wrong."). When you find yourself in a thought trap, do a reality check. Write the thought down, then ask yourself whether it's true. Often, all the *nevers* and *alwayses* reflect how strongly you feel about the situation, not reality. Answer your negative thought with a more positive and realistic one.

■ *Put your expanding mind to good use.* Those new mental powers of yours can help you understand yourself and your needs better. Learning about yourself gives you power. You can't choose what life does to you, but if you know yourself and your dreams, you can choose how to respond.

Changing Relationships

"**M**y mom has this habit of playing 'The Mom' when my friends are over," complains Diana. "She's always popping her head in, asking if we want a soda or if we've heard the latest gossip about some movie star. It's really annoying. But then, if I need her help with something? Say, in deciding what to do for a history report? She'll give me the you're-a-big-girl-so-decide-for-yourself line. It gets me so mad. Why can't she be there when *I* need her to be?"

Diana's mixed feelings about her mom are typical of another change of adolescence: defining new relationships with parents or other adults who take care of us. In childhood, we depend on the adults in our lives for just about everything. But that changes in adolescence. We have ideas of our own about how to dress, whom to see, and how to spend our time. And our parents don't always agree with our choices.

Sometimes you'd think parents want their kids to remain kids. Well, subconsciously they might. You may not think about it, but parents are changing and growing, too. Your adolescence reminds your parents that they too are confronting a new stage of life. They face a task very similar to yours: Just as you're asking "Who am I apart from my parents?" they're asking "Who am I now that my kid has grown?"

Your parents' personal struggle with their own growth might help explain why they sometimes have trouble letting go. It is one reason why they may not always be there when you need them. And you do sometimes need them. After all, taking control of your life is a new business. Like most new things, it's scary as well as exciting. Finding the balance between freedom and dependency that's right for you is tough work. You need to separate, yet you still need the safety of your parents' love. These needs are such opposites that they can confuse and depress you. It's hard to feel two different ways at once. But it's OK. It's normal to have conflicting feelings sometimes.

As you give up your old reliance on adults, you will develop a new reliance on yourself. But most likely you're not there yet. The teen years are a time of transition. You're still forging the new you. As a result, you may be less able to cope with stresses that come along and may find yourself feeling down more often. Learning how to get the support you need from those around you while still building a new, more independent you can help you weather the teenage blues.

Tune In:
Take Care of Your Relationships

One of the things that makes relationships with adults so hard is the feeling that "they just don't understand." Feeling misunderstood is awful and isolating. It is a feeling that often contributes to the blues.

Sometimes, we're so sure no one will understand us that we don't even try to tell others how we feel. Yet knowing that someone *does* understand, that someone cares enough to listen, is often what we need to feel better. Talking with friends certainly helps. But sometimes we need to work out a problem with a parent or other caregiver. Sometimes we need reassurance that the adults in our lives love and respect us. And sometimes we simply need to talk with someone who's already been where we're going — and who remembers what it's like.

Some ways of talking to people make it easier for them to listen. You can learn them. You can ask for the type of listening you need. **Psychiatrist** John B. Livingstone suggests that you try the following.

- Think about what you really want from the other person before you talk. Are you looking for advice? Information? A sympathetic ear? A change in the other person's behavior? Once you've discovered what you want, tell the person in a neutral way. Try to keep annoyance or anger out of your voice.

- Use **"I" statements** when you tell how you're feeling. "I" statements say how you feel without attacking the listener. Here's an example: "When you poke your head in when I'm with friends, I feel childish and embarrassed." Compare this with "You intrude. You're a pest!"

- Try **active listening** — and ask your listener to do the same. When you use this technique, you listen without interrupting and repeat to yourself what the other person is saying. This helps you focus on the other person. Often, feeling listened to makes you feel better even if nothing changes.

- Have people let you know that they're listening accurately by repeating back the idea of what you've said. Do the same for the person with whom you're speaking. This can help avoid misunderstandings.

Unfortunately, talking isn't guaranteed to make you feel better. Sometimes you set out to have a good conversation with a parent only to end up in the same old argument. Or, you may feel lonely or unsatisfied in a conversation and not know why. If this happens to you, don't give up. And don't assume that something is wrong with you. Learning to talk and listen with respect takes time. Someone who interrupts a lot, denies the truth of what you're saying, or jumps in too quickly with suggestions is not really listening. Also, your parents and others can have trouble listening for many reasons that have nothing to do with you. You do your part by being clear about what you think and feel and explaining what you need.

Don't give up on opening lines of communication with someone who is important to you. But don't rely only on that person if he or she can't listen right now. Find someone with whom you can share your feelings. It helps.

Learning to talk and listen with respect takes time, but it's worth it!

Behavior often changes when someone is depressed. A cautious friend may start doing reckless things, for example.

Tara's Blues

Tara hadn't been sleeping well. She'd get up in the middle of the night, heart racing, with a pressure in her head that made her feel like her brain would explode. Her thoughts kept spinning round and round, the same words over and over again: It's not worth it. It's not worth it. It's not worth it. Her mother's nagging was too much. Her father's silences were too much. The loneliness, sadness, and pain were all too much.

Tara didn't know what was wrong with her. But a doctor would have known: Tara was depressed. Someone who's depressed may feel many of the same things as someone who's blue, but the feelings are much stronger, more constant, and longer-lasting. Behavior often changes, too. An outgoing person may withdraw, a cautious friend may start doing reckless things, or someone for whom school always mattered may start skipping classes and not caring about grades.

According to the American Psychiatric Association, someone is depressed when loss of interest or pleasure in almost all activities or feelings of deep sadness last without relief for at least two weeks. Four of the following symptoms must also be present.

- Large weight gain or weight loss (without dieting)
- **Insomnia** or its opposite, excessive sleepiness
- Feelings of worthlessness or guilt ("I'm no good." "I'm not worth loving.")
- Restlessness and irritability or abnormally slow thoughts and body movements (body feels like glue)
- Inability to concentrate or to carry out normal activities, such as doing schoolwork or seeing friends
- Fatigue or loss of energy
- Recurrent thoughts about suicide or death (such as thinking about death as a relief from pain or having recurring images of a specific plan to end it all)

These are the symptoms of depression at any age. In the teen years, depression is sometimes masked. This means that it may show itself in less common ways. Among them are drug and alcohol use; trouble in school, at home, or with the law; withdrawal from social activities; and sulkiness, grouchiness, and over-sensitivity.

Depression, like the blues, can appear to come out of nowhere or can be triggered by a life event. One study found that the death of one's mother or the divorce of one's parents were major depression triggers for teens, although many other losses or rejections can bring on depression, too. Why such experiences trigger depression in one teen but not another is related to how the individual has learned to cope with intense feelings, the person's body chemistry, and life experiences. For example, researchers believe that growing up in a violent or chaotic home can **predispose** a teen to depression. And they know that **heredity** often plays a role: Parents, siblings, and children of a depressed person are four times more likely than a nonrelative to get depressed.

Whatever the cause, depression is a serious illness. The good news is that it can be treated. Scientists know that changes occur in the brain during depression. They have medications that help correct these brain-chemical imbalances. Medicine combined with therapy can help most depressed people recover within a few weeks. Without treatment, depression generally lasts from six months to two years. If you think that you or a friend might be depressed, get help. Talk to a parent, a counselor at school, your doctor, or another adult you trust to take your concerns seriously. The greatest danger of depression is that you will lose hope that things will ever be better. Once hopelessness sets in, so can the belief that life is not worth living.

"I Won't Let You Do This!"

Sherri felt the knot in her stomach tighten as she walked into gym class, the first class she had with Tara. She tried to quiet her breathing as she changed into her gym clothes, all the while checking each class-mate who walked by, hoping to see Tara. Sherri had kept her promise. She hadn't told anyone about Tara's plan. But she also didn't know what had happened to Tara.

Sherri finished changing her clothes. She bent down to tie her sneakers. She was clos-ing her locker as Tara walked by.

"Tara! Wait!" Sherri called, but Tara walked even faster into the girls' bathroom.

By the time Sherri caught up with her, Tara was at the sink, popping a handful of pills into her mouth. Sherri lunged at Tara, knocking the bottle from her hand. Pills fell to the floor like hail. Tara grabbed for the bottle, but Sherri was faster. Crying, she screamed at Tara, "I won't let you do this!"

and ran to get the gym teacher. She didn't think about her promise to Tara. She didn't care. All she cared about was getting help for her friend.

Don't leave your friend to handle depression alone. Suggest that your friend talk to a trusted adult.

A Friend's Cry for Help

Sherri didn't know it, but by showing her the bottle of pills that morning, Tara was really asking for help. Most people who consider suicide have mixed feelings about killing themselves. This doesn't mean that they aren't serious. But it does mean that they may be able to be stopped.

A friend who is suicidal might not come straight out and say, "I want to kill myself," but he or she may drop hints or may behave in life-threatening ways. Here are some things to look and listen for.

■ Comments such as "My family would be better off without me," "I wish I were dead," or "I won't be here for that" (about an event your friend was looking forward to)

■ Dangerous, accident-prone behavior

■ Alcohol or drug abuse

■ Giving away valued possessions

If you suspect that a friend is suicidal, try to find out for sure. Ask your friend these questions: Have things ever seemed as bad as they do now? Have you ever thought of ending it all? Have you thought of how you'd do it? Do you have a plan? The more detailed your friend's plans, the more serious the risk of suicide and the more urgent the need for professional help.

Suggest that your friend talk with a trusted adult — perhaps a teacher, school counselor, or doctor. Calling a suicide prevention center or a pastor or rabbi is another good idea. But don't leave your friend to handle it alone. He or she doesn't necessarily have good judgment right now, but you do. Offer to go with your friend to seek help. Tell him or her that you too are going to talk to an adult who can help.

This isn't easy. Like Sherri, you may have promised to keep a secret. But as Sherri realized, keeping a promise to a friend is less important than saving that friend's life. You can tell your friend, "I know you want me to keep this a secret, but I can't. I care too much about you not to get help." Finding help can also be hard because the adult you turn to might not want to hear what you have to say. He or she might deny or minimize your fears. If this happens, don't assume that you're wrong to be concerned. Turn to someone else: parents, teachers, the school principal, a counselor, or a coach may be able to help. Keep looking until you find someone who will.

And if you are the one who is suicidal, reach out. You may feel like you have no way other than suicide to escape your pain, but you do. When you are depressed, you cannot think clearly or see solutions to your problems. But the depression is an illness. It is not you. You *can* get better, but you need help.

You may feel like you have no other way than suicide to escape your pain, but you do. When you are depressed, you cannot think clearly or see solutions to your problems.

A Final Word

For weeks after Sherri told the gym teacher about Tara and her pills, Tara refused to speak to her. But several months later, Sherri came home to find a present waiting for her on the kitchen table. It was a beautiful ceramic paperweight with the words "Friendship is forever" on it. The note with the gift said, "Thanks. I love you. Tara." Tara had received treatment for her depression. She was feeling better. She was ready to pick up her relationship with her best friend.

Unfortunately, not all stories of depression and suicide end this happily. Some people who commit suicide never drop hints that they intend to kill themselves. Others succeed despite the best efforts of friends or family to stop them. Ultimately, each individual has control of his or her own life. The feelings that lead to suicide are very deep and very private. The best we can do for each other is to offer help.

When someone we love tries to take his or her life, we feel a mix of emotions — rage, guilt, fear, confusion. These feelings are normal and it helps to talk about them. If a student has committed suicide, sometimes the school will arrange for students to meet regularly to talk about what happened. When we share painful feelings, we often drain them of their power to hurt. We discover that other people feel as we do. We discover that we are not alone.

We can feel better after treatment for depression. Tara was able to pick up her relationaship with her best friend after refusing to talk to her for months.

If You'd Like to Learn More

Organizations
The following groups provide information on depression and/or suicide and help for individuals:

National Institute of Mental Health
1-800-421-4211

Boys Town National Hotline (for both girls and boys)
1-800-448-3000

National Foundation for Depressive Illness
1-800-239-1297

National Mental Health Association
1-800-969-6642

Books and Movies
Books and movies can help us understand our feelings better. Here are some that deal with depression and suicide.

Don't Be S.A.D. A Teenage Guide to Handling Stress, Anxiety, and Depression by Susan Newman (New York: Julian Messner, 1991). This discussion of the causes of stress, anxiety, and depression uses teens' first-hand accounts and suggestions of things to do to "move in the right direction" and help readers who are facing similar problems.

Fighting Back: Teenage Depression (Pleasantville, NY: Sunburst Communications, 1991). Through three short stories, this film explores true-to-life crises that can bring on depression and shows how professional counseling can help.

I Can Hear the Mourning Dove by James Bennett (Boston: Houghton Mifflin, 1990). This story tells how a fellow patient helps a girl who is hospitalized for depression get better and get out.

Glossary/Index

active listening: 34 The technique of concentrating on what someone is saying without interrupting.

aerobic exercise: 29 Activity that requires continuous use of oxygen and that benefits the heart and lungs.

depressants: 29 Substances that quiet the central nervous system and have a down effect on mood.

depression: 9 An illness in which a sad mood or loss of pleasure in life, plus other symptoms such as eating and sleeping disorders, lasts without relief for at least two weeks. Depression can lead to suicide and requires professional treatment.

heredity: 39 The traits passed on through the genes from one's ancestors.

"I" statements: 34 Expressions of feelings that start with the word *I*. They state what the speaker is feeling without attacking the listener.

identity crisis: 24 The search for a new sense of self that is typical during adolescence.

insomnia: 38 Inability to sleep. Insomnia can be a sign of depression.

meditation: 29 A relaxation technique in which you breathe deeply and clear your mind of unwanted thoughts by concentrating on a single word or phrase.

predispose: 39 Make more likely to happen.

psychiatrist: 33 A medical doctor who studies how people feel, act, and think, and who treats people who are emotionally troubled.

psychologist: 24 A person trained to understand human behavior and emotions and to help those who are emotionally troubled.

puberty: 26 The time in life when a person is first able to reproduce sexually.

relaxation techniques: 29 Exercises that help you loosen your muscles.

stress: 24 The feeling you get when pressures, events, or other emotions seem like more than you can handle.

yoga: 29 A relaxation exercise involving intense concentration and controlled breathing.